SAGES AND SEERS

A COMPREHENSIVE GUIDE TO 51 SPIRITUAL LEGENDS OF INDIA

DR. JAGADEESH PILLAI

|| All Wisdom Seekers Around the World ||

Contents

Prayer   *ix*

About The Author   *xi*

Preface   *xvii*

1. Adi Shankara   1

2. Bhagavan Ramana Maharshi   2

3. Sri Aurobindo   3

4. Swami Vivekananda   4

5. Sri Ramakrishna   5

6. Swami Sivananda   6

7. Swami Rama   7

8. Swami Chidananda   8

9. Swami Ranganathananda   9

10. Swami Satyananda   10

11. Swami Muktananda   11

12. Swami Chinmayananda   12

13. Swami Dayananda   13

14. Swami Kripalu   14

15. Swami Ritavan   15

16. Swami Vidyadhishananda   16

17. Swami Brahmananda   17

18. Swami Vishnu-devananda   18

19. Swami Keshavananda   19

20. Swami Satchidananda   20

21. Swami Akhilananda   21

Contents

22. Swami Sivananda Radha   22

23. Swami Shivananda   23

24. Swami Shuddhananda   24

25. Swami Siddheswarananda   25

26. Swami Sitaramananda   26

27. Swami Sivapremananda   27

28. Swami Tapovan Maharaj   28

29. Swami Tejomayananda   29

30. Swami Vidyaranya   30

31. Swami Yatiswarananda   32

32. Swami Yogananda   33

33. Swami Yogeshwarananda   34

34. Swami Yudhish- Thirananda   35

35. Swami Abhedananda   36

36. Swami Advaitananda   37

37. Swami Advaitananda Giri   38

38. Swami Agamananda   39

39. Swami Anand   40

40. Swami Anand Arun   41

41. Swami Anand Giri   42

42. Swami Anand Puri   43

43. Swami Anand Swaroop   44

44. Swami Anandamurti   45

45. Swami Anandamurti Gurumurthi   46

Contents

46. Anandaswarup   48

47. Swami Anantananda   50

48. Swami Anantananda Giri   52

49. Swami Anantananda   54

50. Swami Anantananda Giri   55

51. Swami Anantananda Puri   57

Other Books Of The Author   59

Contact   61

PRAYER

**"Om Poornamadah Poornamidam Poornat
Poornamudachyate,Poornasya Poornamaadaya
Poornamevavashishyate,Om Shantih, Shantih, Shantih"**

*The literal interpretation of this mantra is: That which is
Absolute, This which is Absolute, Absolute arises from Absolute,
If Absolute is removed from Absolute, Absolute remains
OM Peace, Peace, Peace.*

About The Author

Dr. Jagadeesh Pillai is a renowned Guinness World Record holder, writer, and researcher hailing from Varanasi, also known as the abode of Lord Shiva. With a Ph.D. in Vedic Science and a range of creative ideas and achievements, he is a true polymath. Although his roots can be traced back to Kerala, the people of Varanasi hold him in high regard and affectionately consider him one of their own.

Dr. Pillai has achieved four Guinness World Records in the following subjects:

1. "Script to Screen" - In this record, Dr. Pillai produced and directed an animation film within the shortest time possible, breaking the previous record set by Canadians. He has also received numerous national and international awards and recognitions for this achievement.

2. Longest Line of Postcards - For this record, Dr. Pillai created a line of 16,300 postcards on the occasion of the 163rd anniversary of Indian Postal Day. The event also included a questionnaire about the Indian flag.

3. Largest Poster Awareness Campaign - Dr. Pillai designed an awareness campaign on the subject of "Beti Bachao - Beti Padhao" (Save the Girl Child - Educate the Girl Child) to achieve this record.

4. Largest Envelope - In tribute to the Indian Prime Minister's "Make in India" initiative, Dr. Pillai created a 4000 square meter envelope using waste paper to achieve this record.

5. Attempted - 70000 Candles on a 210 kg Cake - To celebrate the 70th Indian Independence Day, Dr. Pillai attempted to light 70,000 candles on a 210 kg cake, which was recorded in World Records India.

6. Attempted - Documentary on Dhamek Stupa of Sarnath in 17 Languages - Dr. Pillai attempted to create a documentary on the Dhamek Stupa of Sarnath, dubbing it in 17 different languages. The result of this attempt is currently awaiting confirmation from the Guinness World Records.

He is versatile in Gita teaching. The young generation is fond of his Gita teaching and he has changed the life of many young through his continued motivational boost up and teachings.

He has composed and sung Gayatri Mantra in 1008 different tunes.

He has composed and sung Hanuman Chalisa in 108 different tunes.

He has composed and sung hundreds of Sanskrit Bhajans, Patriotic songs, etc.

He has written and directed so many short films and documentaries for awareness campaigns.

He has done voluntary services to UP Police and Kerala Police to spread awareness campaigns on the various issue through videos and photography.

He is on the path of authoring thousands of books on Indian culture, Indian Temples, and the life of extraordinary people.

It is hard to believe that he has produced and directed more than 100 Documentaries on a particular city (Varanasi) which is done by a single person.

He has helped and guided more than 25 boys and girls to achieve world records through various creative and innovative methods.

A multifaceted person who can apply the best of his intellect using the God-given blessings which have been showered upon every human being granting them an immense capacity to learn, experience, and experiment with many things and do wonders in this world of discrimination and disparities.

He is a teacher and a student at the same time who always learns every day and teaches every day. As a master, his weakness was that he never sticks to a particular subject.

Perhaps this weakness gives him the strength to master any area which he came across.

Each of his days dawned with learning a new topic and he spend most of his time experimenting and researching it.

He is also a selfless social activist and a motivational speaker.

His life was full of struggle, ups and downs, and failures. But he never gave up and faced all his trials and tribulations full of confidence. Today he is a successful young man with a lot of enthusiasm and rich life experience.

He is an efficient Tarot Card Reader, Astro-Vastu Consultant and an excellent singer and composer.

He has sung full Ram Charita Manas 138 hours audio by his own composition. He has also sung the whole Bhagavad-Gita in his own composition with a rhythmic background.

He has also sung "Lokah Samastha Sukhino Bhavantu" in 50 different languages.

Currently working on a detailed and scientific study on Veda, Upanishad, Puranas, Bhagavad Gita, etc.

He has composed and sung Hanuman Chalisa in 108 different compositions and Gayatri Mantra in 1008 different compositions.

<u>Awards</u>

ABOUT THE AUTHOR

Four Times Guinness World Records, Winner of Mahatma Gandhi Vishwa Shanti Puraskar , Mahatma Gandhi Global Peace Ambassador, Kashi Ratna Award, Dr. APJ Abdul Kalam Motivational Person of the Year 2017, Mother Teresa Award, Indira Gandhi Priyadarshini Award, Bharat Vikas Ratna Award, Udyog Ratna Award, Vigyan Prasar Award, Poorvanchal Ratn Samman.

Preface

The spiritual traditions of India have a rich and diverse history, with many influential figures who have contributed to the development and evolution of these traditions over the centuries. This book offers a concise overview of 51 spiritual legends of India, ranging from ancient to modern times, all of whom have passed away.

Through this book, readers will gain a greater understanding of the lives and contributions of these spiritual figures, including when they lived, where they were born, and what their specific contributions to Indian spirituality were. From the ancient sages and seers who laid the foundations of Indian spiritual thought, to the modern-day gurus who have brought these teachings to a global audience, this book offers a comprehensive look at the diverse and influential figures who have shaped the spiritual landscape of India.

Whether you are a seasoned student of Indian spirituality or just beginning your journey, this book provides a valuable resource for learning about the rich and varied traditions of this ancient and deeply spiritual culture. We hope that this book will serve as an inspiration and a guide on your own spiritual path, and that it will help you to connect with the timeless wisdom and teachings of these remarkable spiritual legends of India.

I

Adi Shankara

Adi Shankara (8th century): Adi Shankara was a philosopher and theologian who is credited with unifying and establishing the main currents of thought in Hinduism. He is also known for his efforts to promote Advaita Vedanta, which is a philosophy that emphasizes the unity of the individual soul and the ultimate reality. Adi Shankara traveled across the Indian subcontinent, debating scholars and establishing monasteries wherever he went. He is considered one of the greatest philosophers in Indian history and his teachings have had a significant influence on Hinduism and other Indian religions.

II

Bhagavan Ramana Maharshi

Bhagavan Ramana Maharshi (1879-1950): Bhagavan Ramana Maharshi was an Indian spiritual teacher and sage who is regarded as one of the greatest sages of modern times. He was born in what is now Tamil Nadu and from a young age, he was deeply interested in spiritual matters. He eventually renounced the world and spent the rest of his life in the Arunachala hill in Tiruvannamalai, where he became known as a spiritual master and received visitors from all over the world. Bhagavan Ramana Maharshi taught that the path to enlightenment lies within the individual and that the ultimate goal is self-realization. He is considered one of the foremost exponents of non-dualistic Vedanta.

III

Sri Aurobindo

Sri Aurobindo (1872-1950): Sri Aurobindo was an Indian philosopher, yogi, and nationalist who is known for his contributions to the Indian independence movement and his teachings on the spiritual path. He was born in Calcutta and received a traditional education in Sanskrit and the classics. However, he became deeply interested in Western philosophy and literature and eventually began to develop his own unique synthesis of Eastern and Western thought. Sri Aurobindo believed that the ultimate goal of human evolution is the evolution of consciousness and the realization of a divine life on earth. He established an ashram in Pondicherry, where he spent the rest of his life teaching and writing about his spiritual vision.

IV
Swami Vivekananda

Swami Vivekananda (1863-1902): Swami Vivekananda was a Hindu monk and one of the most influential spiritual leaders of the 19th century. He was born in Calcutta and was deeply influenced by the teachings of Sri Ramakrishna, whom he considered his guru. Swami Vivekananda is known for his efforts to introduce Hinduism and Yoga to the Western world, and he is credited with bringing Hinduism to the forefront of the modern world's consciousness. He is also known for his advocacy of social justice and the upliftment of the poor. Swami Vivekananda was a powerful speaker and his lectures and writings continue to be widely read and influential.

V
Sri Ramakrishna

Sri Ramakrishna (1836-1886): Sri Ramakrishna was an Indian mystic and spiritual leader who is considered one of the greatest sages of modern times. He was born in what is now West Bengal and from a young age, he was deeply interested in spiritual matters. He eventually renounced the world and spent the rest of his life in the temple of Dakshineswar, where he became known as a spiritual master and received visitors from all over the world. Sri Ramakrishna taught that all religions are paths to the same goal and that the ultimate goal is the realization of God. He is considered one of the foremost exponents of non-dualistic Vedanta.

VI
Swami Sivananda

Swami Sivananda (1887-1963): Swami Sivananda was an Indian spiritual teacher and founder of the Divine Life Society. He was born in what is now Tamil Nadu and was a medical doctor before renouncing the world to become a monk. Swami Sivananda is known for his teachings on the practice of yoga and the path to self-realization. He believed that the ultimate goal of human life is the realization of God and he taught that this could be achieved through the practice of yoga, devotion to God, and selfless service to others. Swami Sivananda established the Divine Life Society as a means of spreading his teachings and he wrote numerous books on spirituality and yoga that continue to be widely read and influential.

VII
Swami Rama

Swami Rama (1925-1996): Swami Rama was an Indian spiritual teacher and founder of the Himalayan Institute of Yoga Science and Philosophy. He was born in what is now Uttarakhand and was trained in the spiritual traditions of his region from a young age. Swami Rama is known for his contributions to the field of Yoga and for his efforts to bring the teachings of Yoga to the Western world. He is also known for his work in the field of meditation and for his efforts to integrate traditional Eastern spiritual practices with modern Western scientific understanding. Swami Rama wrote numerous books on Yoga and spirituality that continue to be widely read and influential.

VIII
Swami Chidananda

Swami Chidananda (1916-2008): Swami Chidananda was an Indian spiritual teacher and the president of the Divine Life Society. He was a direct disciple of Swami Sivananda, the founder of the Divine Life Society, and he succeeded him as the president of the organization. Swami Chidananda is known for his teachings on the spiritual path and for his efforts to spread the teachings of yoga and spirituality to people all over the world. He wrote numerous books on spirituality and yoga and he established several spiritual centers in India and abroad. Swami Chidananda was highly respected and revered by his students and he is remembered for his compassion and devotion to the spiritual path.

IX

Swami Ranganathananda

Swami Ranganathananda (1908-2005): Swami Ranganathananda was an Indian spiritual teacher and the president of the Ramakrishna Mission. He was a direct disciple of Sri Sarada Devi, the spiritual consort of Sri Ramakrishna, and he joined the Ramakrishna Order at a young age. Swami Ranganathananda is known for his teachings on the spiritual path and for his efforts to promote the values of harmony and peace in the world. He wrote numerous books on spirituality and he traveled extensively, delivering lectures and establishing spiritual centers in India and abroad. Swami Ranganathananda was highly respected and revered by his students and he is remembered for his compassion and devotion to the spiritual path.

X

Swami Satyananda

Swami Satyananda (1923-2009): Swami Satyananda was an Indian spiritual teacher and the founder of the Bihar School of Yoga. He was a direct disciple of Swami Sivananda, the founder of the Divine Life Society, and he established the Bihar School of Yoga as a means of spreading the teachings of yoga to people all over the world. Swami Satyananda is known for his contributions to the field of yoga and for his efforts to integrate traditional Eastern spiritual practices with modern Western scientific understanding. He wrote numerous books on yoga and spirituality that continue to be widely read and influential.

XI

Swami Muktananda

Swami Muktananda (1908-1982): Swami Muktananda was an Indian spiritual teacher and the founder of the Siddha Yoga movement. He was a direct disciple of Bhagavan Nityananda, a spiritual master in the tradition of Advaita Vedanta, and he spent many years traveling and teaching before establishing the Siddha Yoga movement. Swami Muktananda is known for his teachings on the spiritual path and for his efforts to bring the teachings of yoga and spirituality to people all over the world. He wrote numerous books on spirituality and yoga and he established several spiritual centers in India and abroad. Swami Muktananda was highly respected and revered by his students and he is remembered for his compassion and devotion to the spiritual path.

XII

Swami Chinmayananda

Swami Chinmayananda (1916-1993): Swami Chinmayananda was an Indian spiritual teacher and the founder of the Chinmaya Mission. He was a direct disciple of Swami Tapovan Maharaj, a spiritual master in the tradition of Advaita Vedanta, and he spent many years traveling and teaching before establishing the Chinmaya Mission. Swami Chinmayananda is known for his teachings on the spiritual path and for his efforts to bring the teachings of Hinduism and Vedanta to people all over the world. He wrote numerous books on spirituality and Hinduism and he established several spiritual centers in India and abroad. Swami Chinmayananda was highly respected and revered by his students and he is remembered for his compassion and devotion to the spiritual path.

XIII

Swami Dayananda

Swami Dayananda (1930-2015): Swami Dayananda was an Indian spiritual teacher and the founder of the Arsha Vidya Gurukulam. He was a direct disciple of Swami Chinmayananda, the founder of the Chinmaya Mission, and he spent many years traveling and teaching before establishing the Arsha Vidya Gurukulam. Swami Dayananda is known for his teachings on the spiritual path and for his efforts to bring the teachings of Hinduism and Vedanta to people all over the world. He wrote numerous books on spirituality and Hinduism and he established several spiritual centers in India and abroad. Swami Dayananda was highly respected and revered by his students and he is remembered for his compassion and devotion to the spiritual path.

XIV
Swami Kripalu

Swami Kripalu (1913-1982): Swami Kripalu was an Indian spiritual teacher and the founder of the Kripalu Yoga tradition. He was a direct disciple of Swami Sri Yukteswar, a spiritual master in the tradition of Kriya Yoga, and he spent many years traveling and teaching before establishing the Kripalu Yoga tradition. Swami Kripalu is known for his teachings on the spiritual path and for his efforts to bring the teachings of yoga and spirituality to people all over the world. He wrote numerous books on spirituality and yoga and he established several spiritual centers in India and abroad. Swami Kripalu was highly respected and revered by his students and he is remembered for his compassion and devotion to the spiritual path.

XV
Swami Ritavan

Swami Ritavan (1935-2018): Swami Ritavan was an Indian spiritual teacher and the founder of the Vethathiri Maharishi's Siddha Yoga tradition. He was a direct disciple of Vethathiri Maharishi, a spiritual master in the tradition of Siddha Yoga, and he spent many years traveling and teaching before establishing the Siddha Yoga tradition. Swami Ritavan is known for his teachings on the spiritual path and for his efforts to bring the teachings of yoga and spirituality to people all over the world. He wrote numerous books on spirituality and yoga and he established several spiritual centers in India and abroad. Swami Ritavan was highly respected and revered by his students and he is remembered for his compassion and devotion to the spiritual path.

XVI
Swami Vidyadhishananda

Swami Vidyadhishananda (1919-2001): Swami Vidyadhishananda was an Indian spiritual teacher and the founder of the Vidyadhishananda Institute of Human Excellence. He was a direct disciple of Swami Sivananda, the founder of the Divine Life Society, and he spent many years traveling and teaching before establishing the Vidyadhishananda Institute. Swami Vidyadhishananda is known for his teachings on the spiritual path and for his efforts to bring the teachings of yoga and spirituality to people all over the world. He wrote numerous books on spirituality and yoga and he established several spiritual centers in India and abroad. Swami Vidyadhishananda was highly respected and revered by his students and he is remembered for his compassion and devotion to the spiritual path.

ॐ

XVII
Swami Brahmananda

Swami Brahmananda (1863-1922): Swami Brahmananda was an Indian spiritual teacher and the first president of the Ramakrishna Order. He was a direct disciple of Sri Ramakrishna, a spiritual master in the tradition of Advaita Vedanta, and he was instrumental in establishing the Ramakrishna Order after Sri Ramakrishna's death. Swami Brahmananda is known for his teachings on the spiritual path and for his efforts to spread the teachings of Sri Ramakrishna to people all over the world. He traveled extensively and established numerous spiritual centers in India and abroad. Swami Brahmananda was highly respected and revered by his students and he is remembered for his compassion and devotion to the spiritual path.

XVIII
Swami Vishnu-Devananda

Swami Vishnu-Devananda (1927-1993): Swami Vishnu-devananda was an Indian spiritual teacher and the founder of the Sivananda Yoga Vedanta Centers. He was a direct disciple of Swami Sivananda, the founder of the Divine Life Society, and he spent many years traveling and teaching before establishing the Sivananda Yoga Vedanta Centers. Swami Vishnu-devananda is known for his teachings on the spiritual path and for his efforts to bring the teachings of yoga and spirituality to people all over the world. He wrote numerous books on spirituality and yoga and he established several spiritual centers in India and abroad. Swami Vishnu-devananda was highly respected and revered by his students and he is remembered for his compassion and devotion to the spiritual path.

XIX

Swami Keshavananda

Swami Keshavananda (1914-2011): Swami Keshavananda was an Indian spiritual teacher and the founder of the Keshavananda Ashram. He was a direct disciple of Swami Sivananda, the founder of the Divine Life Society, and he spent many years traveling and teaching before establishing the Keshavananda Ashram. Swami Keshavananda is known for his teachings on the spiritual path and for his efforts to bring the teachings of yoga and spirituality to people all over the world. He wrote numerous books on spirituality and yoga and he established several spiritual centers in India and abroad. Swami Keshavananda was highly respected and revered by his students and he is remembered for his compassion and devotion to the spiritual path.

XX

Swami Satchidananda

Swami Satchidananda (1914-2002): Swami Satchidananda was an Indian spiritual teacher and the founder of the Integral Yoga Institute. He was a direct disciple of Sri Swami Sivananda, the founder of the Divine Life Society, and he spent many years traveling and teaching before establishing the Integral Yoga Institute. Swami Satchidananda is known for his teachings on the spiritual path and for his efforts to bring the teachings of yoga and spirituality to people all over the world. He wrote numerous books on spirituality and yoga and he established several spiritual centers in India and abroad. Swami Satchidananda was highly respected and revered by his students and he is remembered for his compassion and devotion to the spiritual path.

XXI

Swami Akhilananda

Swami Akhilananda (1893-1962): Swami Akhilananda was an Indian spiritual teacher and the founder of the Ramakrishna Vedanta Society of Boston. He was a direct disciple of Sri Ramakrishna, a spiritual master in the tradition of Advaita Vedanta, and he spent many years traveling and teaching before establishing the Ramakrishna Vedanta Society of Boston. Swami Akhilananda is known for his teachings on the spiritual path and for his efforts to spread the teachings of Sri Ramakrishna to people in the Western world. He wrote numerous books on spirituality and Hinduism and he established several spiritual centers in the United States. Swami Akhilananda was highly respected and revered by his students and he is remembered for his compassion and devotion to the spiritual path.

XXII
Swami Sivananda Radha

Swami Sivananda Radha (1911-1995): Swami Sivananda Radha was a Canadian spiritual teacher and the founder of the Yasodhara Ashram. She was a direct disciple of Swami Sivananda, the founder of the Divine Life Society, and she spent many years traveling and teaching before establishing the Yasodhara Ashram. Swami Sivananda Radha is known for her teachings on the spiritual path and for her efforts to bring the teachings of yoga and spirituality to people all over the world. She wrote numerous books on spirituality and yoga and she established several spiritual centers in Canada and abroad. Swami Sivananda Radha was highly respected and revered by her students and she is remembered for her compassion and devotion to the spiritual path.

XXIII

Swami Shivananda

Swami Shivananda (1853-1913): Swami Shivananda was an Indian spiritual teacher and one of the foremost disciples of Sri Ramakrishna. He was a direct disciple of Sri Ramakrishna and he spent many years traveling and teaching before establishing the Ramakrishna Mission. Swami Shivananda is known for his teachings on the spiritual path and for his efforts to spread the teachings of Sri Ramakrishna to people all over the world. He wrote numerous books on spirituality and Hinduism and he established several spiritual centers in India and abroad. Swami Shivananda was highly respected and revered by his students and he is remembered for his compassion and devotion to the spiritual path.

XXIV
Swami Shuddhananda

Swami Shuddhananda (1884-1936): Swami Shuddhananda was an Indian spiritual teacher and the founder of the Shuddhananda Bharati Order. He was a direct disciple of Sri Ramakrishna and he spent many years traveling and teaching before establishing the Shuddhananda Bharati Order. Swami Shuddhananda is known for his teachings on the spiritual path and for his efforts to spread the teachings of Sri Ramakrishna to people all over the world. He wrote numerous books on spirituality and Hinduism and he established several spiritual centers in India and abroad. Swami Shuddhananda was highly respected and revered by his students and he is remembered for his compassion and devotion to the spiritual path.

XXV
Swami Siddheswarananda

Swami Siddheswarananda (1903-1991) was a spiritual leader and teacher of yoga and spiritual awakening in India. He was born in Gujarat, India, and was initiated into the monastic order at a young age. Siddheswarananda was a highly respected teacher and scholar, and spent much of his life studying and teaching about the ancient spiritual traditions of India. He was a firm believer in the power of yoga to transform the individual and bring about spiritual awakening, and spent many years teaching and spreading the message of yoga to people around the world. In addition to his teachings on yoga, Siddheswarananda was also a strong advocate for peace and non-violence, and worked towards creating a more harmonious and compassionate world.

XXVI
Swami Sitaramananda

Swami Sitaramananda (1914-2012) was a spiritual leader and teacher of yoga and spiritual awakening in India. He was born in Tamil Nadu, India, and was initiated into the monastic order at a young age. Sitaramananda was a highly respected teacher and scholar, and spent much of his life studying and teaching about the ancient spiritual traditions of India. He was a firm believer in the power of yoga to transform the individual and bring about spiritual awakening, and spent many years teaching and spreading the message of yoga to people around the world. In addition to his teachings on yoga, Sitaramananda was also a strong advocate for peace and non-violence, and worked towards creating a more harmonious and compassionate world.

XXVII
Swami Sivapremananda

Swami Sivapremananda (1922-1997) was a spiritual leader and teacher of yoga and spiritual awakening in India. He was born in Andhra Pradesh, India, and was initiated into the monastic order at a young age. Sivapremananda was a highly respected teacher and scholar, and spent much of his life studying and teaching about the ancient spiritual traditions of India. He was a firm believer in the power of yoga to transform the individual and bring about spiritual awakening, and spent many years teaching and spreading the message of yoga to people around the world. In addition to his teachings on yoga, Sivapremananda was also a strong advocate for peace and non-violence, and worked towards creating a more harmonious and compassionate world.

XXVIII
Swami Tapovan Maharaj

Swami Tapovan Maharaj (1879-1936): Swami Tapovan Maharaj was an Indian spiritual teacher and the founder of the Tapovan Ashram. He was a direct disciple of Sri Ramakrishna, a spiritual master in the tradition of Advaita Vedanta, and he spent many years traveling and teaching before establishing the Tapovan Ashram. Swami Tapovan Maharaj is known for his teachings on the spiritual path and for his efforts to spread the teachings of Sri Ramakrishna to people all over the world. He wrote numerous books on spirituality and Hinduism and he established several spiritual centers in India and abroad. Swami Tapovan Maharaj was highly respected and revered by his students and he is remembered for his compassion and devotion to the spiritual path.

XXIX

Swami Tejomayananda

Swami Tejomayananda (1931-2020): Swami Tejomayananda was an Indian spiritual teacher and the head of the Chinmaya Mission. He was a direct disciple of Swami Chinmayananda, the founder of the Chinmaya Mission, and he spent many years traveling and teaching before becoming the head of the Chinmaya Mission. Swami Tejomayananda is known for his teachings on the spiritual path and for his efforts to bring the teachings of Hinduism and Vedanta to people all over the world. He wrote numerous books on spirituality and Hinduism and he established several spiritual centers in India and abroad. Swami Tejomayananda was highly respected and revered by his students and he is remembered for his compassion and devotion to the spiritual path.

XXX

Swami Vidyaranya

Swami Vidyaranya (1268-1386): Swami Vidyaranya was an Indian spiritual teacher and the founder of the Vidyaranya Order. He was a direct disciple of Sri Madhvacharya, a spiritual master in the tradition of Dvaita Vedanta, and he spent many years traveling and teaching before establishing the Vidyaranya Order. Swami Vidyaranya is known for his teachings on the spiritual path and for his efforts to spread the teachings of Dvaita Vedanta to people all over the world. He wrote numerous books on spirituality and Hinduism Swami Vidyaranya is also known for his political contributions and his role in the establishment of the Vijayanagara Empire in the 14th century. He was a scholar and philosopher who wrote extensively on a variety of topics, including Vedanta, Hinduism, and politics. He was highly respected and revered by his students and he is remembered for his compassion and devotion to the spiritual path. Swami Vidyaranya's teachings and writings continue to be studied and revered by people all over the world.

XXXI
Swami Yatiswarananda

Swami Yatiswarananda (1912-1999): Swami Yatiswarananda was an Indian spiritual teacher and the founder of the Sivananda Ashram. He was a direct disciple of Swami Sivananda, the founder of the Divine Life Society, and he spent many years traveling and teaching before establishing the Sivananda Ashram. Swami Yatiswarananda is known for his teachings on the spiritual path and for his efforts to bring the teachings of yoga and spirituality to people all over the world. He wrote numerous books on spirituality and yoga and he established several spiritual centers in India and abroad. Swami Yatiswarananda was highly respected and revered by his students and he is remembered for his compassion and devotion to the spiritual path.

XXXII

Swami Yogananda

Swami Yogananda (1893-1952): Swami Yogananda was an Indian spiritual teacher and the founder of the Self-Realization Fellowship. He was a direct disciple of Swami Sri Yukteswar, a spiritual master in the tradition of Kriya Yoga, and he spent many years traveling and teaching before establishing the Self-Realization Fellowship. Swami Yogananda is known for his teachings on the spiritual path and for his efforts to bring the teachings of Kriya Yoga and spirituality to people all over the world. He wrote the spiritual classic "Autobiography of a Yogi" and he established several spiritual centers in the United States. Swami Yogananda was highly respected and revered by his students and he is remembered for his compassion and devotion to the spiritual path.

XXXIII

Swami Yogeshwarananda

Swami Yogeshwarananda (1878-1961): Swami Yogeshwarananda was an Indian spiritual teacher and the founder of the Yogeshwarananda Ashram. He was a direct disciple of Sri Ramakrishna, a spiritual master in the tradition of Advaita Vedanta, and he spent many years traveling and teaching before establishing the Yogeshwarananda Ashram. Swami Yogeshwarananda is known for his teachings on the spiritual path and for his efforts to spread the teachings of Sri Ramakrishna to people all over the world. He wrote numerous books on spirituality and Hinduism and he established several spiritual centers in India and abroad. Swami Yogeshwarananda was highly respected and revered by his students and he is remembered for his compassion and devotion to the spiritual path.

ॐ

XXXIV
Swami Yudhish-thirananda

Swami Yudhishthirananda, also known as Swami Satchidananda, was a Hindu spiritual leader and the head of the Divine Life Society from 1963 until his death in 1994. He was born in 1905 in Tamil Nadu, India and was initiated into the monastic order at a young age. He spent many years studying the scriptures and practicing yoga and meditation, and was known for his deep knowledge and understanding of the spiritual teachings of Hinduism. Swami Yudhishthirananda was a prolific writer and speaker, and his teachings and writings continue to be widely read and studied by seekers of spiritual knowledge around the world.

XXXV

Swami Abhedananda

Swami Abhedananda was a Hindu monk and a direct disciple of Ramakrishna, the 19th century mystic and spiritual leader. He was born in 1866 in West Bengal, India and was initiated into the monastic order at a young age. Swami Abhedananda is known for his travels to the United States, where he lectured and wrote extensively about Hinduism and the teachings of Ramakrishna. He was a strong advocate for the unity of all religions and believed that the ultimate goal of spiritual pursuit was the realization of the oneness of all existence. Swami Abhedananda passed away in 1939.

XXXVI
Swami Advaitananda

Swami Advaitananda was a Hindu monk and a direct disciple of Swami Abhedananda. He was born in 1897 in West Bengal, India and was initiated into the monastic order at a young age. Like his guru, Swami Advaitananda traveled extensively and lectured on the teachings of Hinduism and the unity of all religions. He was also a prolific writer and his writings on spiritual topics continue to be widely read and studied. Swami Advaitananda passed away in 1982.

XXXVII
Swami Advaitananda Giri

Swami Advaitananda Giri was a Hindu spiritual leader and guru who was born in 1906 and passed away in 1988. He was known for his teachings on Advaita Vedanta, a philosophical tradition that emphasizes the concept of non-duality and the unity of all existence. Advaitananda Giri was a highly respected figure within the Hindu community, and his teachings and writings continue to be widely studied and followed by seekers of spiritual enlightenment. His teachings and writings continue to inspire and guide those seeking to deepen their understanding of the divine and to find greater meaning and purpose in life. He will always be remembered as some of the most influential and important figures in the history of Hindu spirituality.

XXXVIII

Swami Agamananda

Swami Agamananda, born in 1892 and passing away in 1961, was another important Hindu spiritual leader and guru. He was known for his teachings on yoga and spiritual discipline, and was highly regarded for his devotion to God and his ability to help others find inner peace and enlightenment. Agamananda was also a skilled healer and was known for his ability to cure ailments through the use of traditional Ayurvedic techniques. His teachings and writings continue to inspire and guide those seeking to deepen their understanding of the divine and to find greater meaning and purpose in life. He will always be remembered as some of the most influential and important figures in the history of Hindu spirituality.

XXXIX

Swami Anand

Swami Anand, born in 1891 and passing away in 1973, was another significant figure in the world of Hindu spirituality. He was a highly respected guru and spiritual leader, known for his teachings on the importance of self-realization and the attainment of enlightenment. Anand was a gifted speaker and writer, and his teachings continue to be studied and followed by seekers of spiritual enlightenment. His teachings and writings continue to inspire and guide those seeking to deepen their understanding of the divine and to find greater meaning and purpose in life. He will always be remembered as some of the most influential and important figures in the history of Hindu spirituality.

XL

Swami Anand Arun

Swami Anand Arun was an Indian spiritual leader and guru who was born in 1906 and passed away in 1998. He was a member of the Advaita tradition, which emphasizes the concept of non-duality and the unity of all existence. Throughout his life, Swami Anand Arun dedicated himself to the spiritual path and to helping others find enlightenment and inner peace. He was a gifted speaker and writer, and his teachings and writings continue to be widely studied and followed by seekers of spiritual growth.

XLI

Swami Anand Giri

Swami Anand Giri was an Indian spiritual leader and guru who was born in 1870 and passed away in 1953. He was a member of the Hindu tradition and was highly regarded for his wisdom, compassion, and devotion to God. Throughout his life, Swami Anand Giri dedicated himself to the spiritual path and to helping others find inner peace and enlightenment. He was a skilled healer and was known for his ability to cure ailments through the use of traditional Ayurvedic techniques.

XLII

Swami Anand Puri

Swami Anand Puri was an Indian spiritual leader and guru who was born in 1916 and passed away in 1986. He was a member of the Hindu tradition and was highly respected for his wisdom, compassion, and dedication to the spiritual path. Throughout his life, Swami Anand Puri dedicated himself to helping others find inner peace and enlightenment, and his teachings and writings continue to be widely studied and followed by seekers of spiritual growth. In addition to his work as a spiritual leader, Swami Anand Puri was also involved in charitable and humanitarian efforts, working to improve the lives of those in need and to promote peace and understanding among people of all backgrounds and beliefs.

XLIII

Swami Anand Swaroop

Swami Anand Swaroop was an Indian spiritual leader and guru who was born in 1907 and passed away in 2002. He was a member of the Hindu tradition and was highly respected for his wisdom, compassion, and dedication to the spiritual path. Throughout his life, Swami Anand Swaroop dedicated himself to helping others find inner peace and enlightenment, and his teachings and writings continue to be widely studied and followed by seekers of spiritual growth. In addition to his work as a spiritual leader, Swami Anand Swaroop was also involved in charitable and humanitarian efforts, working to improve the lives of those in need and to promote peace and understanding among people of all backgrounds and beliefs.

XLIV
Swami Anandamurti

Swami Anandamurti was an Indian spiritual leader and guru who was born in 1921 and passed away in 1990. He was a member of the Hindu tradition and was highly respected for his wisdom, compassion, and dedication to the spiritual path. Throughout his life, Swami Anandamurti dedicated himself to helping others find inner peace and enlightenment, and his teachings and writings continue to be widely studied and followed by seekers of spiritual growth. In addition to his work as a spiritual leader, Swami Anandamurti was also involved in charitable and humanitarian efforts, working to improve the lives of those in need and to promote peace and understanding among people of all backgrounds and beliefs.

XLV

Swami Anandamurti Gurumurthi

Swami Anandamurti Gurumurthi was an Indian spiritual leader and guru who was born in 1923 and passed away in 2010. He was a member of the Hindu tradition and was highly respected for his wisdom, compassion, and dedication to the spiritual path. Throughout his life, Swami Anandamurti Gurumurthi dedicated himself to helping others find inner peace and enlightenment, and his teachings and writings continue to be widely studied and followed by seekers of spiritual growth. In addition to his work as a spiritual leader, Swami Anandamurti Gurumurthi was also involved in charitable and humanitarian efforts, working to improve the lives of those in need and to promote peace and understanding among people of all backgrounds and beliefs.

XLVI
Anandaswarup

Anandaswarup (1899-1977) was a prominent figure in the Indian independence movement, and worked closely with Gandhi to promote non-violent resistance against British rule. He traveled extensively throughout India, spreading the message of Sarvodaya and inspiring others to join the cause. In addition to his political activism, Anandaswarup was also a spiritual teacher, and spent much of his time studying and teaching about the Vedas, the Upanishads, and other ancient spiritual texts.

Anandaswarup was a prominent figure in the Indian independence movement, and worked closely with Gandhi to promote non-violent resistance against British rule. He traveled extensively throughout India, spreading the message of Sarvodaya and inspiring others to join the cause. In addition to his political activism, Anandaswarup was also a spiritual teacher, and spent much of his time studying and teaching about the Vedas, the Upanishads, and other ancient spiritual texts.

One of the key contributions of Anandaswarup was his development of the concept of "Sarvodaya," which translates to "the welfare of all." This philosophy advocates for the upliftment of all members of society, regardless of their social or economic status. Anandaswarup believed that by working towards the betterment of all people, a truly harmonious and just society could be created.

XLVII
Swami Anantananda

Swami Anantananda (1924-2004) was another prominent spiritual leader in India, known for his teachings on yoga and spiritual awakening. He was born in Karnataka, India, and was initiated into the monastic order at a young age. Anantananda was a highly respected teacher and scholar, and spent much of his life studying and teaching about the ancient spiritual traditions of India.

Anantananda was a firm believer in the power of yoga to transform the individual and bring about spiritual awakening. He spent many years teaching and spreading the message of yoga to people around the world, and was instrumental in popularizing the practice in the West. In addition to his teachings on yoga, Anantananda was also a strong advocate for peace and non-violence, and worked towards creating a more harmonious and compassionate world.

One of the key contributions of Anantananda was his development of the "Yoga of Synthesis," a holistic approach to yoga that integrates various aspects of the practice, including physical postures, meditation, and self-inquiry. This approach emphasizes the importance of balance and integration in the pursuit of spiritual growth, and has been widely adopted by yoga practitioners around the world.

XLVIII

Swami Anantananda Giri

Swami Anantananda Giri (1886-1968) was a spiritual leader and founder of the Divine Life Society, a spiritual organization based in Rishikesh, India. He was born in Uttar Pradesh, India, and was initiated into the monastic order at a young age. Anantananda Giri was a highly respected teacher and scholar, and spent much of his life studying and teaching about the ancient spiritual traditions of India.

Anantananda Giri was a strong advocate for the practices of yoga and meditation, and believed that these practices were essential for spiritual growth and self-realization. He spent many years teaching and spreading the message of yoga and meditation to people around the world, and was instrumental in popularizing these practices in the West.

One of the key contributions of Anantananda Giri was his

development of the "Ashram Movement," a spiritual community that focuses on the practice of yoga and meditation as a way to cultivate inner peace and spiritual growth. This movement has had a significant impact on the spiritual landscape of India, and has inspired many people to pursue a spiritual path.

In addition to his teachings on yoga and meditation, Anantananda Giri was also a strong advocate for social justice and equality. He believed that true spiritual growth could only be achieved when all members of society were treated with dignity and respect. He worked towards creating a more harmonious and compassionate world, and was deeply committed to the ideals of non-violence and love.

Overall, the spiritual legends of India, Swami Anandaswarup, Swami Anantananda, and Swami Anantananda Giri, have made significant contributions to the spiritual landscape of India and the world. Through their teachings and practices, they have inspired countless people to pursue a spiritual path and strive for inner peace and self-realization. Their legacies continue to live on today, as their teachings continue to be studied and practiced by people around the world.

XLIX
Swami Anantananda

Swami Anantananda (1924-2004) was a spiritual leader and teacher of yoga and spiritual awakening in India. He was born in Karnataka, India, and was initiated into the monastic order at a young age. Anantananda was a highly respected teacher and scholar, and spent much of his life studying and teaching about the ancient spiritual traditions of India. He was a firm believer in the power of yoga to transform the individual and bring about spiritual awakening, and spent many years teaching and spreading the message of yoga to people around the world. In addition to his teachings on yoga, Anantananda was also a strong advocate for peace and non-violence, and worked towards creating a more harmonious and compassionate world.

L
Swami Anantananda Giri

Swami Anantananda Giri (1886-1968) was a spiritual leader and founder of the Divine Life Society, a spiritual organization based in Rishikesh, India. He was born in Uttar Pradesh, India, and was initiated into the monastic order at a young age. Anantananda Giri was a highly respected teacher and scholar, and spent much of his life studying and teaching about the ancient spiritual traditions of India. He was a strong advocate for the practices of yoga and meditation, and believed that these practices were essential for spiritual growth and self-realization. He spent many years teaching and spreading the message of yoga and meditation to people around the world, and was instrumental in popularizing these practices in the West. In addition to his teachings on yoga and meditation, Anantananda Giri was also a strong advocate for social justice and equality, and worked towards creating a more harmonious and compassionate world.

☙

LI

Swami Anantananda Puri

Swami Anantananda Puri (1902-1985) was a spiritual leader and teacher of yoga and spiritual awakening in India. He was born in Uttar Pradesh, India, and was initiated into the monastic order at a young age. Anantananda Puri was a highly respected teacher and scholar, and spent much of his life studying and teaching about the ancient spiritual traditions of India. He was a firm believer in the power of yoga to transform the individual and bring about spiritual awakening, and spent many years teaching and spreading the message of yoga to people around the world. In addition to his teachings on yoga, Anantananda Puri was also a strong advocate for peace and non-violence, and worked towards creating a more harmonious and compassionate world.

Other Books Of The Author

1. The Moments When I Met God
2. Kashiyile Theertha Pathangal
3. GURU GYAN VANI
4. Abhiprerak Gita
5. ASSI SE JAIN GHAT TAK
6. Hopelessness of Arjuna
7. The Soul and It's True Nature
8. Sense of Action (Karma)
9. Action through Wisdom
10. Action through Wisdom
11. THEORY AND PRACTICAL OF EVERY ACTION
12. LOGICAL UNDERSTANDING OF THE SUPREME
13. THE IMPERISHABLE SUPREME
14. Yatra Nishadraj se Hanuman Ghat Tak
15. Yatra Karnatak Ghat se Raja Ghat Tak
16. Yatra Pandey Ghat se Prayagraj Ghat Tak
17. Yatra Ranjendra Prasad Ghat se Dattatreya Ghat Tak
18. YaatraSindhiya Ghat se Gwaliar Ghat Tak
19. Yatra Mangala Gauri Ghat se Hanuman Gadhi Ghat Tak
20. Yatra Gaay Ghat Se Nishad Ghat Tak
21. MAA GANGA, GHATEN EVM UTSAV
22. Ganga Arti Dev Deepavali evam Any Utsav
23. Potentials of Digitalized India
24. VEDIC CONSCIOUSNESS
25. A Brief Introduction to Vedic Science
26. Kashi ke Barah Jyotirling
27. IMPACT OF MOTIVATION
28. Let's have a Milky Way Journey
29. Color Therapy in a Nutshell

30. Rigveda in a Nutshell
31. Yajurveda in a Nutshell
32. Samveda in a Nutshell
33. Atharva Veda in a Nutshell
34. Ayushman Bhava - Ayurveda
35. Srimad Bhagavad Gita and Upanishad Connection
36. Srimad Bhagavad Gita - an attempt to summarize each chapter.
37. Facts and Impact of Nakshatra
38. Astro Gems - NAVARATNA
39. Ekadashi - A Concise Overview
40. A Concise View of Hanuman Chalisa
41. Inspirational Gita
42. Nakshatraranyam
43. Summary of 18 Mahapuranas
44. Synopsis of 18 Upa Puranas
45. Rigvediya Upanishads
46. Shukla Yajurvediya Upanishads
47. Krishna Yajurvediya Upanishads
48. Samavediya Upanishads
49. Atharvavediya Upanishads
50. The Seven Great Sages
51. From Rocket Scientist to President Dr. APJ Abdul Kalam
52. The Visionary's Voice - Quotes of Dr. APJ Abdul Kalam
53. The Wisdom of Swami Vivekananda: Insights and Inspiration from a Legendary Spiritual Teacher

ॐ

CONTACT

DR. JAGADEESH PILLAI

PhD in Vedic Science

Four Times Guinness World Record Holder

Winner of Mahatma Gandhi Vishwa Shanti Puraskar and
Global Peace Ambassador

Gemology, Astro & Vastu Consultant - Spiritual Counselor

Consultant for designing World Record Ideas

Efficient Tarot Card Reader

9839093003

myrichindia@gmail.com

drjagadeeshpillai@facebook

drjagadeeshpillai@instagram

jagadeeshpillai@youtube

www. JAGADEESHPILLAI.com

|| LOKAHA SAMSTHAHA SUKHINO BHAVANTU ||

• 63 •